AF189432

Impressum
Verlag: BABADADA GmbH, Nedderfeld 112 , 22529 Hamburg
Geschäftsführer / Verlagsleitung: Harald Hof
Druck: Books on Demand GmbH, In de Tarpen 42, 22848 Norderstedt

Imprint
Publisher: BABADADA GmbH, Nedderfeld 112 , 22529 Hamburg, Germany
Managing Director / Publishing direction: Harald Hof
Print: Books on Demand GmbH, In de Tarpen 42, 22848 Norderstedt

school
scol

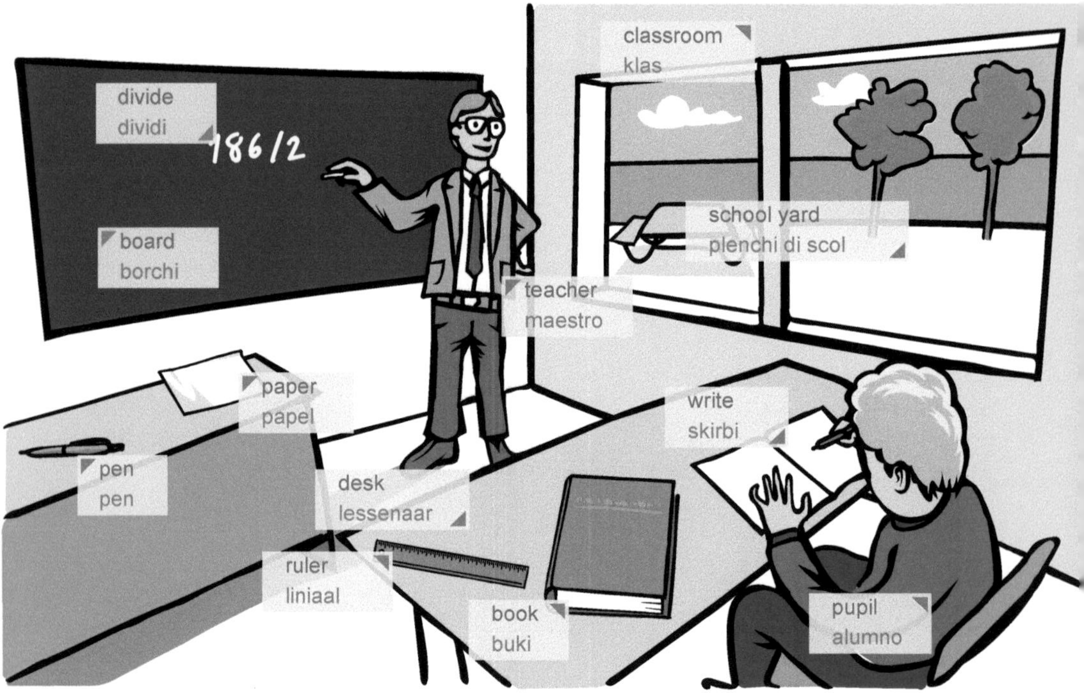
classroom
klas
divide
dividi
186/2
board
borchi
school yard
plenchi di scol
teacher
maestro
paper
papel
write
skirbi
pen
pen
desk
lessenaar
ruler
liniaal
book
buki
pupil
alumno

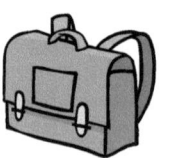

satchel

tas di scol

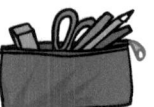

pencil case

etui

pencil

potlood

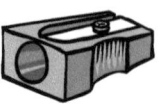

pencil sharpener

slijper

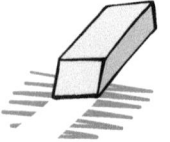

rubber

gum

drawing pad

buki di pinta

drawing
....
pintura

paintbrush
....
cuashi

paint box
....
caha di verf

scissors
....
sker

glue
....
lijm

exercise book
....
schrift

homework
....
huiswerk

number
....
number

add
....
suma

subtract
....
kita

multiply
....
multiplica

calculate
....
conta

letter
....
letter

alphabet
....
alfabet

word
....
palabra

text

texto

read

lesa

chalk

krijt

lesson

les

register

klassenboek

examination

examen

certificate

diploma

school uniform

uniform di scol

education

estudio

encyclopedia

enciclopedia

university

universidad

microscope

microscop

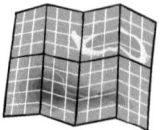

map

mapa

waste-paper basket

bari di sushi

travel
biahamento

hotel
hotel
Grand
hostel
posada
ROOMS
EXCHANGE
currency exchange office
oficina di cambio
suitcase
maleta
car
auto

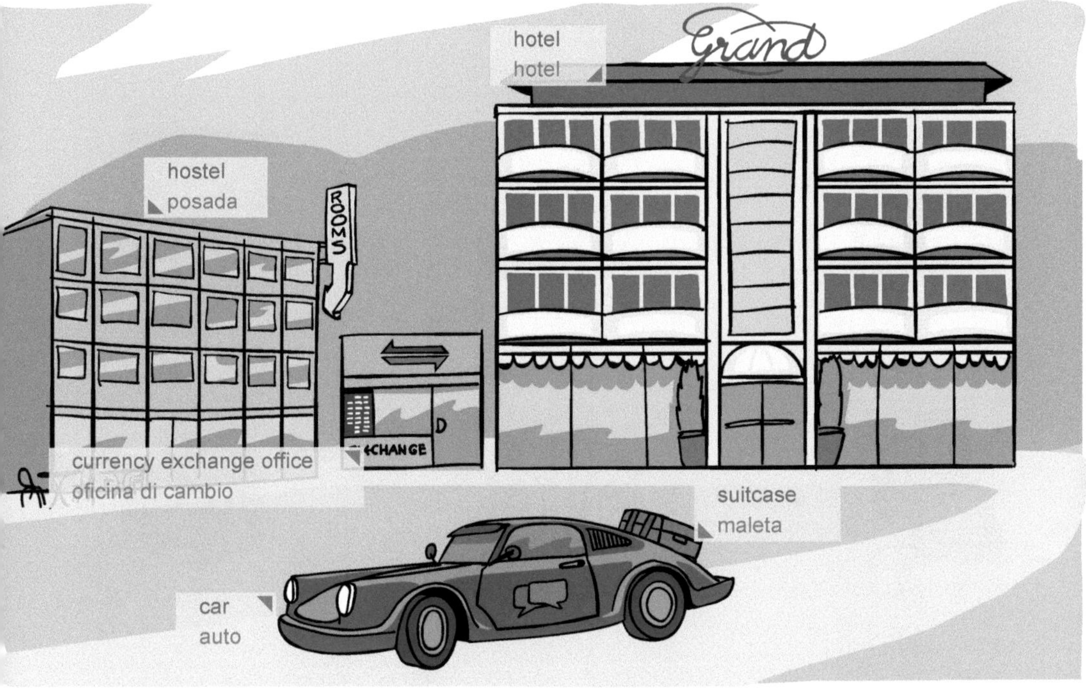

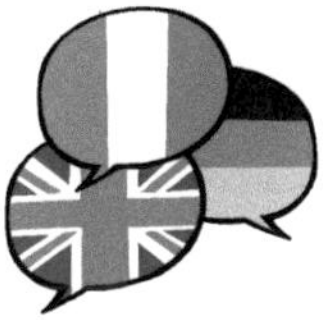

language
idioma

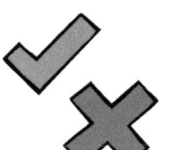

yes / no
si / no

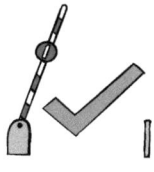

Okay
bon

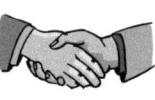

hello
hallo

translator
tolk

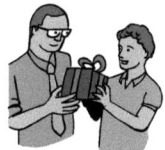

Thank you
masha danki

how much is...?

Cuanto esaki ta costa?

I don´t get it

Mi no ta compronde

problem

problema

Good evening!

bon nochi

Good morning!

Bon dia!

Good night!

Bon nochi!

goodbye

ayo

direction

direccion

luggage

maleta

bag

handbag

backpack

rugtas

guest

huesped

room

camber

sleeping bag

slaapzak

tent

tent

tourist information

informacion pa turista

beach

lama

credit card

credit card

breakfast

desayuno

lunch

cuminda di merdia

dinner

cuminda di anochi

Ticket

carchi

elevator

cabe'i boto

stamp

stampia

border

grens

customs

duana

embassy

embahada

visa

visa

passport

paspoort

transport

transport

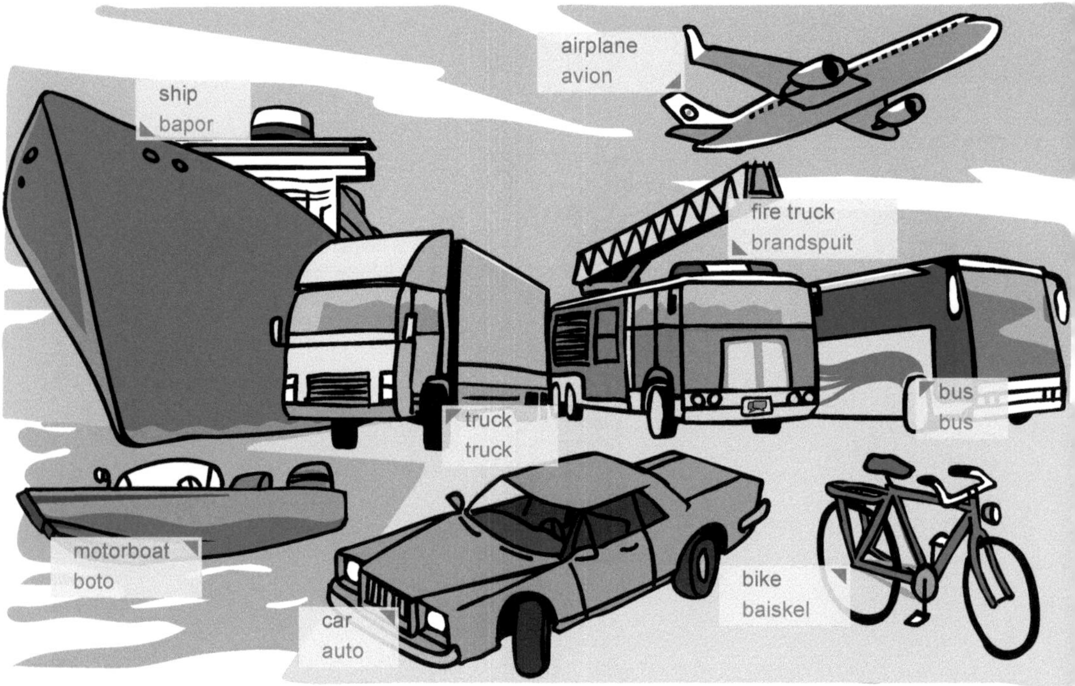
airplane
avion
ship
bapor
fire truck
brandspuit
bus
bus
truck
truck
motorboat
boto
bike
baiskel
car
auto

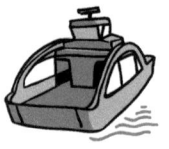

ferry

ferry

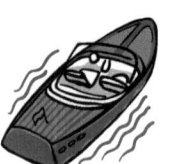

boat

boto

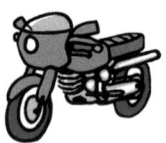

motorbike

brommer

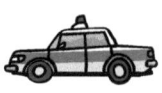

police car

auto di polis

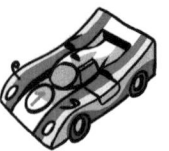

racing car

auto di careda

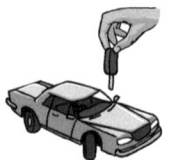

rental car

auto di huur

car sharing

car sharing

tow truck

takelwagen

garbage truck

dump truck

engine

motor

fuel

gasolin

fuel station

pomp di gasolin

traffic sign

borchi di trafico

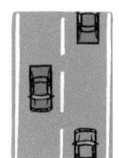

traffic

trafico

traffic jam

fila

parking lot

parkeerplaats

train station

stacion di trein

tracks

riel

train

trein

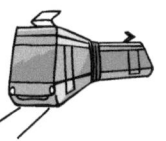

tram

tram

wagon

wagon

helicopter

helicopter

airport

aeropuerto

tower

toren

passenger

pasahero

container

container

carton

caha di carton

cart

garoshi

basket

macutu

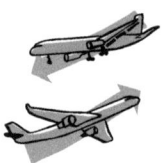

take off / land

lanta / baha

city

ciudad

village

pueblo

city center

centro di ciudad

house

cas

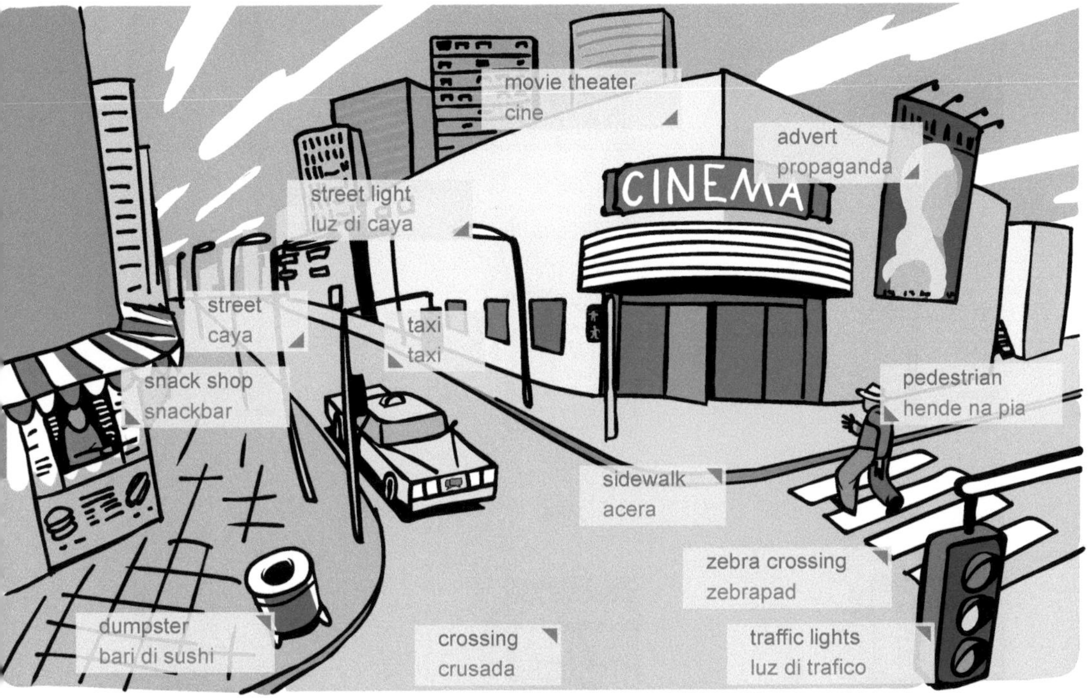

movie theater
cine
advert
propaganda
CINEMA
street light
luz di caya
street
caya
taxi
taxi
snack shop
snackbar
pedestrian
hende na pia
sidewalk
acera
zebra crossing
zebrapad
dumpster
bari di sushi
crossing
crusada
traffic lights
luz di trafico

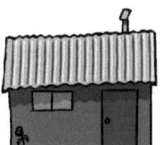

hut

hut

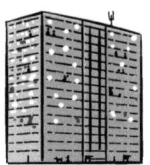

apartment

flat

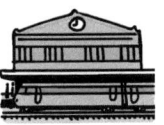

train station

stacion di trein

city hall

stadhuis

MUSEUM

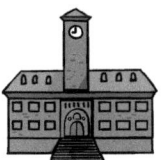

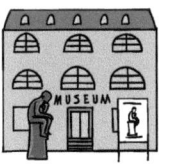

museum

museo

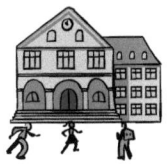

school

scol

university

universidad

bank

banco

hospital

hospital

hotel

hotel

pharmacy

botica

office

oficina

book shop

boekhandel

shop

tienda

flower shop

floresteria

supermarket

supermarket

market

mercado

department store

department store

fishmonger's shop

bendedo di pisca

mall

shopping center

harbor

haf

park
park

bench
banki

bridge
brug

stairs
trapi

subway
metro

tunnel
tunnel

bus stop
parada di bus

bar
bar

restaurant
restaurant

postbox
postbox

street sign
borchi di nomber di caya

parking meter
parkeermeter

zoo
parke di bestia

swimming pool
piscina

mosque
moskee

farm
cunucu

pollution
polucion

cemetery
santana

church
misa

playground
speelplaats

temple
tempel

landscape

paisahe

leaf
blachi

signpost
borchi di direccion

path
caminda

meadow
sabana

stone
piedra

tree
palo

hiker
keirodo

river
riu

grass
yerba

flower
flor

valley

vallei

hill

sero

lake

lago

forest

mondi

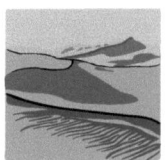

desert

desierto

volcano

volcan

castle

kasteel

rainbow

arco iris

mushroom

paddenstoel

palm tree

palma

mosquito

sangura

fly

musca

ant

vruminga

bee

bij

spider

haraña

landscape - paisahe

beetle
tor

frog
dori

squirrel
eekhoorn

hedgehog
porcospina

hare
coneu

owl
shoco

bird
parha

swan
zwaan

boar
porco di mondi

deer
bina

moose
eland

dam
dam

wind turbine
molina di biento

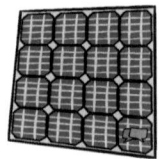

solar panel
panel solar

climate
clima

restaurant
restaurant

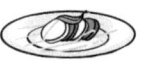

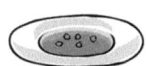

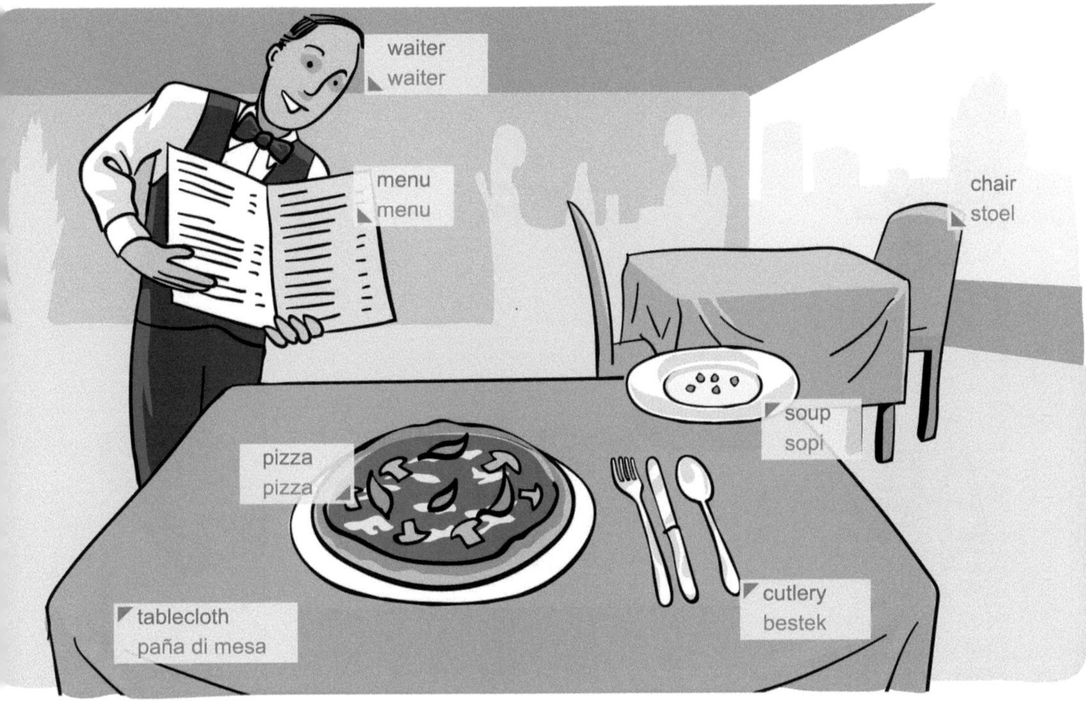
waiter
waiter
menu
menu
chair
stoel
soup
sopi
pizza
pizza
cutlery
bestek
tablecloth
paña di mesa

starter

aperitivo

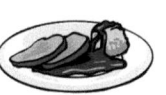

main course

cuminda principal

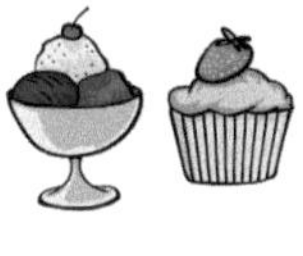

dessert

dessert

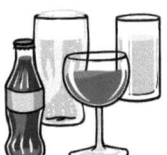

drinks

bebida

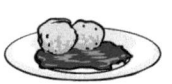

food

cuminda

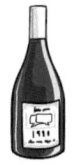

bottle

boter

fast food

fastfood

street food

streetfood

teapot

canica di te

sugar bowl

pochi di sucu

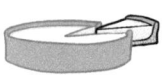

portion

porcion

espresso machine

espressomachine

high chair

stoel di mucha

bill

cuenta

tray

hasechi

knife

cuchiu

fork

forki

spoon

cuchara

teaspoon

telep

serviette

napkin

glass

glas

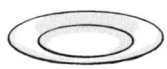

plate

tayo

soup plate

tayo di sopi

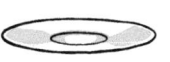

saucer

scoter

sauce

saus

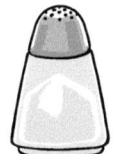

salt shaker

pochi di salo

pepper mill

mulina di peper

vinegar

binager

oil

azeta

spices

specerij

ketchup

ketchup

mustard

mosterd

mayonnaise

mayonaise

supermarket

supermarket

special offer
oferta special
FOR
customer
cliente
dairy products
producto lacteo
fruit
fruta
shopping cart
garoshi di compra

BUTCHERS

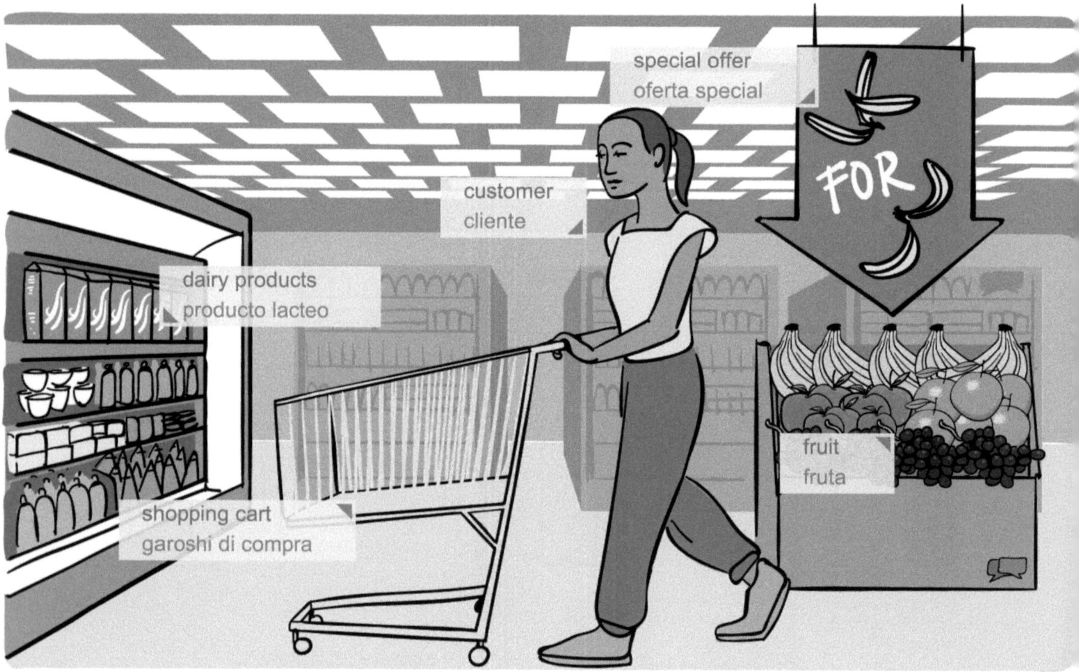

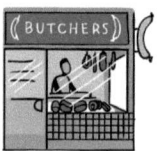

butcher's shop

carniceria

BAKERY

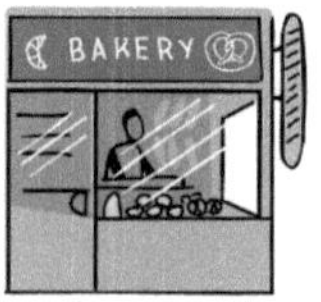

bakery

panaderia

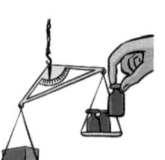

weigh

pisa

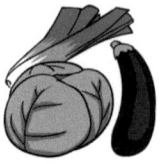

vegetables

berdura

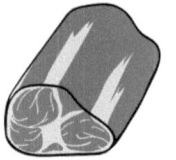

meat

carni

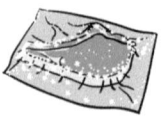

frozen food

frozen food

cold cuts

beleg di carni

canned food

cuminda di bleki

detergent

detergente na puiro

candy

mangel

household products

producto pa cas

cleaning products

articulo di limpiesa

sales representative

bendedo

cash register

cahero

cashier

cahero

shopping list

lista di compra

opening hours

orario

wallet

cartera

credit card

credit card

bag

tas

plastic bag

saco di plastic

water
awa

juice
juice

milk
lechi

coke
cola

wine
biña

beer
cerbes

alcohol
alcohol

cocoa
chocomel

tea
te

coffee
koffie

espresso
espresso

cappuccino
cappuccino

banana

bacoba

apple

appel

orange

apelsina

melon

milon

lemon

lamunchi

carrot

wortel

garlic

conoflok

bamboo

bambu

onion

siboyo

mushroom

mushroom

nuts

noot

noodles

pasta

spaghetti

spaghetti

rice

aros

salad

salada

fries

batata hasa

fried potatoes

batata hasa

pizza

pizza

hamburger

hamburger

sandwich

sandwich

escalope

cutlet

ham

ham

salami

salami

sausage

soseishi

chicken

galiña

roast

hasa

fish

pisca

porridge oats
papa

muesli
müsli

cornflakes
cornflakes

flour
hariña

croissant
croissant

bread roll
pan rondo

bread
pan

toast
toast

cookies
cuki

butter
manteca

curd
kwark

cake
bolo

egg
webo

fried egg
webo hasa

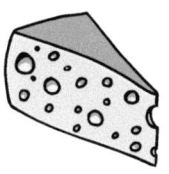

cheese
keshi

ice cream

ijscream

sugar

sucu

honey

honing

jelly

jam

nougat cream

pasta di chuculati

curry

curry

farm

cunucu

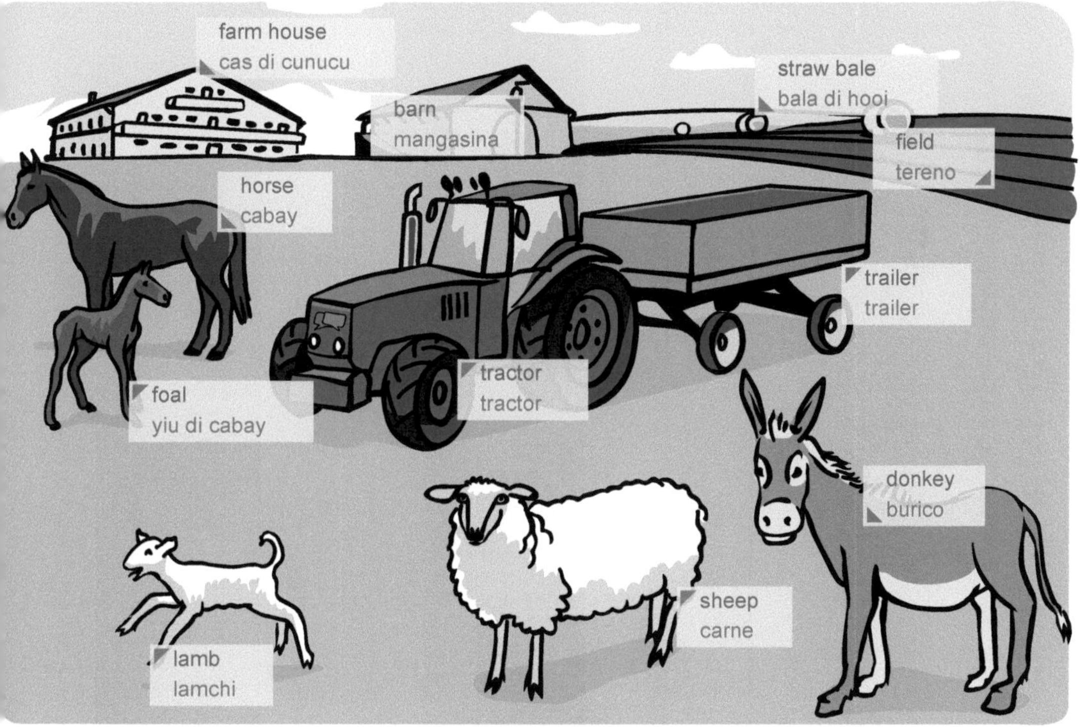
farm house
cas di cunucu
barn
mangasina
straw bale
bala di hooi
field
tereno
horse
cabay
trailer
trailer
tractor
tractor
foal
yiu di cabay
donkey
burico
sheep
carne
lamb
lamchi

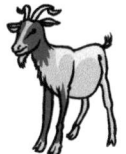

goat

cabrito

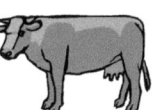

cow

baca

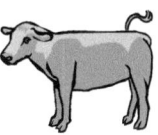

calf

bishe

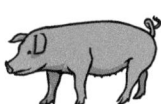

pig

porco

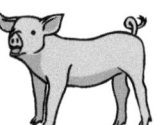

piglet

yiu di porco

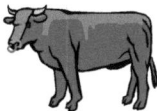

bull

toro

goose
gans

duck
pato

chick
puyito

hen
galiña

cockerel
gay

rat
djaca

cat
pushi

mouse
raton

ox
toro

dog
cacho

dog house
cas di cacho

garden hose
slang pa muha mata

watering can
gieter

scythe
herment pa corta yerbe

plow
ploeg

sickle

garabati

hoe

chapi

pitchfork

forki pa coy hooi

axe

hacha

pushcart

garetia

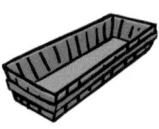

trough

pesebre

milk can

canica di lechi

sack

saco

fence

heki

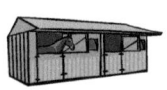

stable

stal

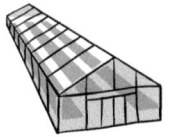

greenhouse

greenhouse

soil

suela

seed

simia

fertilizer

mest

combine harvester

mashin di cosecha

harvest

cosecha

harvest

cosecha

yams

yams

wheat

trigo

soya

soya

potato

batata

corn

maishi

rapeseed

canola

fruit tree

palo di fruta

manioc

yuca

grain

grano

house

cas

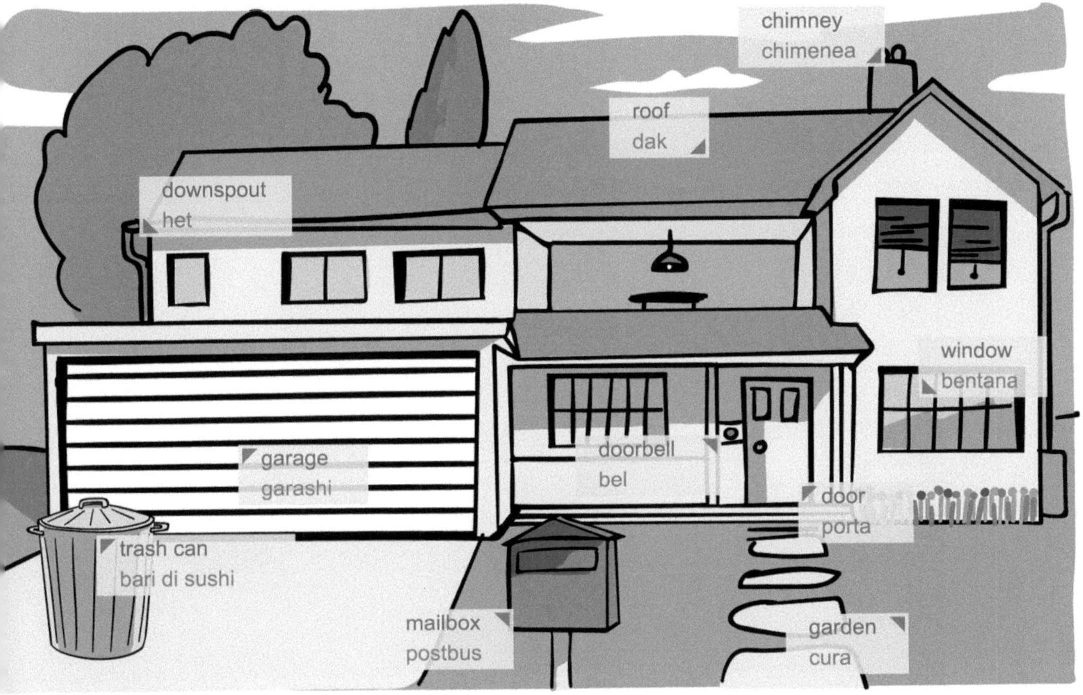
chimney
chimenea
roof
dak
downspout
het
window
bentana
garage
garashi
doorbell
bel
door
porta
trash can
bari di sushi
mailbox
postbus
garden
cura

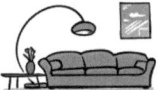

living room

sala

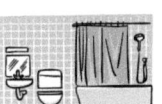

bathroom

baño

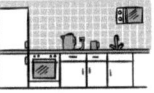

kitchen

cushina

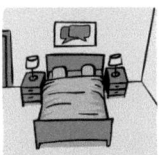

bedroom

camber

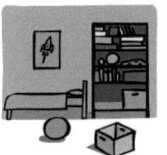

kids room

camber di mucha

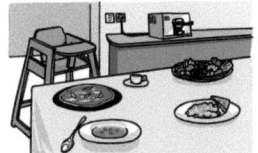

dining room

comedo

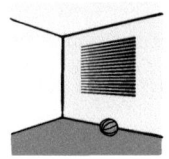

floor

suela

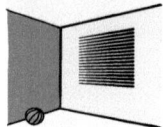

wall

muraya

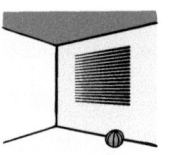

ceiling

blafon

cellar

bodega

sauna

sauna

balcony

balcon

terrace

terasa

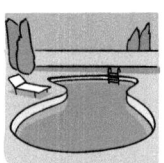

pool

piscina

lawn mower

mashin di corta yerba

sheet

laken

bedspread

bedsprei

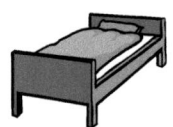

bed

cama

broom

basora

bucket

hemchi

switch

switch

living room
sala

wallpaper
papel pa papela
picture
potret
lamp
lampi
shelf
reki
cabinet
cashi
television
television
fireplace
fogon
flower
flor
cushion
cusinchi
sofa
sofa
vase
vaas
remote control
remote control

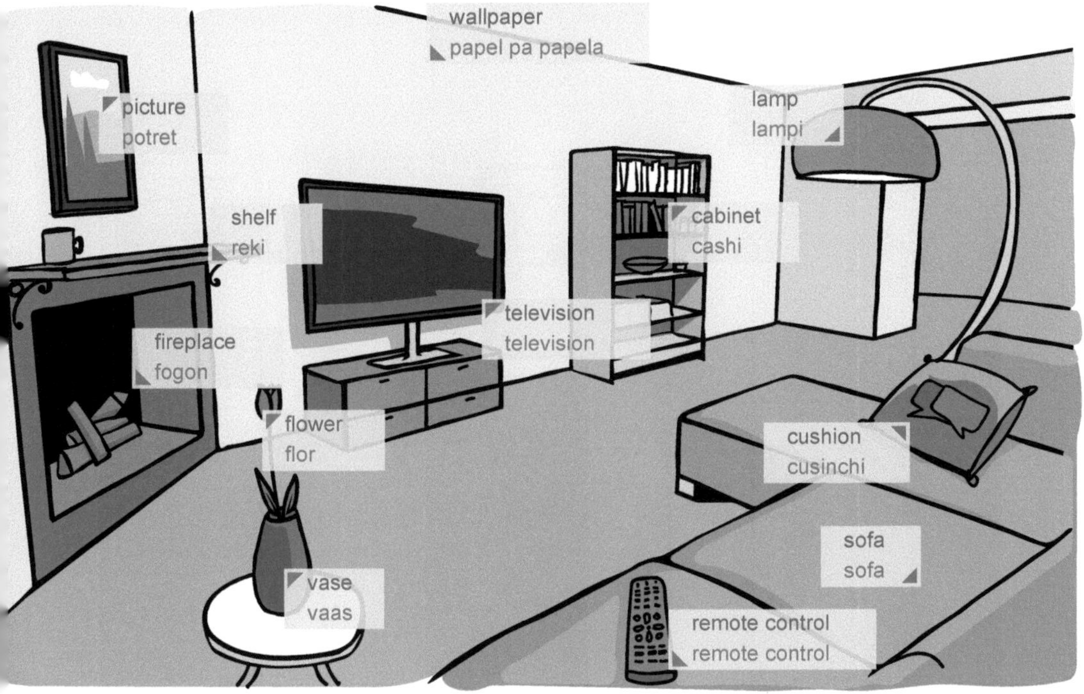

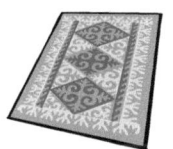

carpet
tapijt

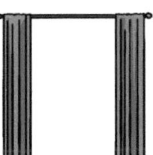

drape
cortina

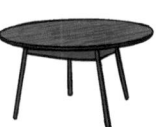

table
mesa

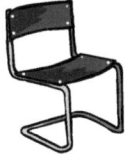

chair
stoel

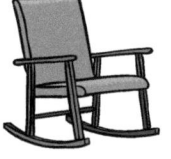

rocking chair
stoel di zoya

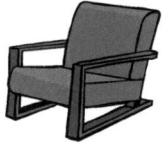

armchair
stoel

book

buki

blanket

dekel

decoration

decoracion

firewood

palo pa kima

film

film

stereo system

stereoset

key

yabi

newspaper

corant

painting

cuadra

poster

poster

radio

radio

notebook

blocnote

vacuum cleaner

stofzuiger

cactus

cadushi

candle

bela

kitchen
cushina

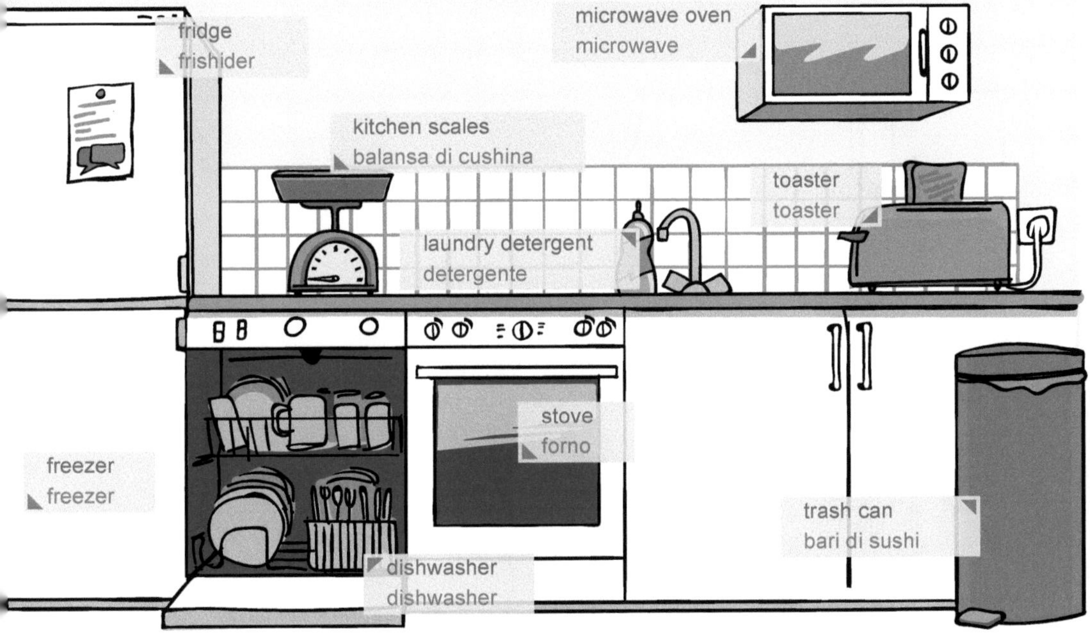
fridge
frishider
microwave oven
microwave
kitchen scales
balansa di cushina
toaster
toaster
laundry detergent
detergente
stove
forno
freezer
freezer
trash can
bari di sushi
dishwasher
dishwasher

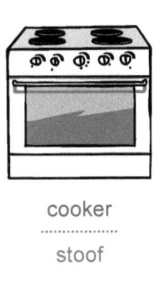

cooker

stoof

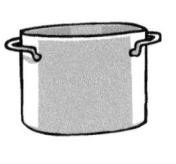

pot

wea

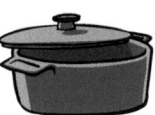

cast-iron pot

wea di hero

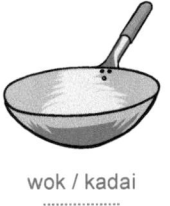

wok / kadai

wok

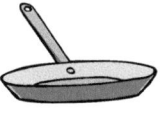

pan

planchi

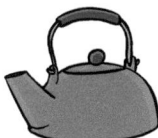

kettle

ketel

steamer

steamer

baking tray

teblachi pa horna

crockery

servies

mug

beker

bowl

conchi

chopsticks

chopstick

ladle

cuchara di sopi

spatula

spatula

whisk

garde

strainer

scurido

sieve

colado

grater

raspa

mortar

fenso

barbecue

barbecue

fireplace

candela

chopping board

planki pa corta

rolling pin

rostok

corkscrew

kurkentrek

can

bleki

can opener

cos di habri bleki

oven cloth

pannenlap

sink

wasbak

brush

skeiro

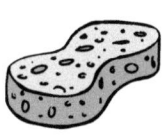

sponge

spons

blender

blender

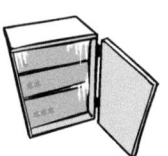

deep freezer

freezer

baby bottle

tetero

tap

cranchi

bathroom
baño

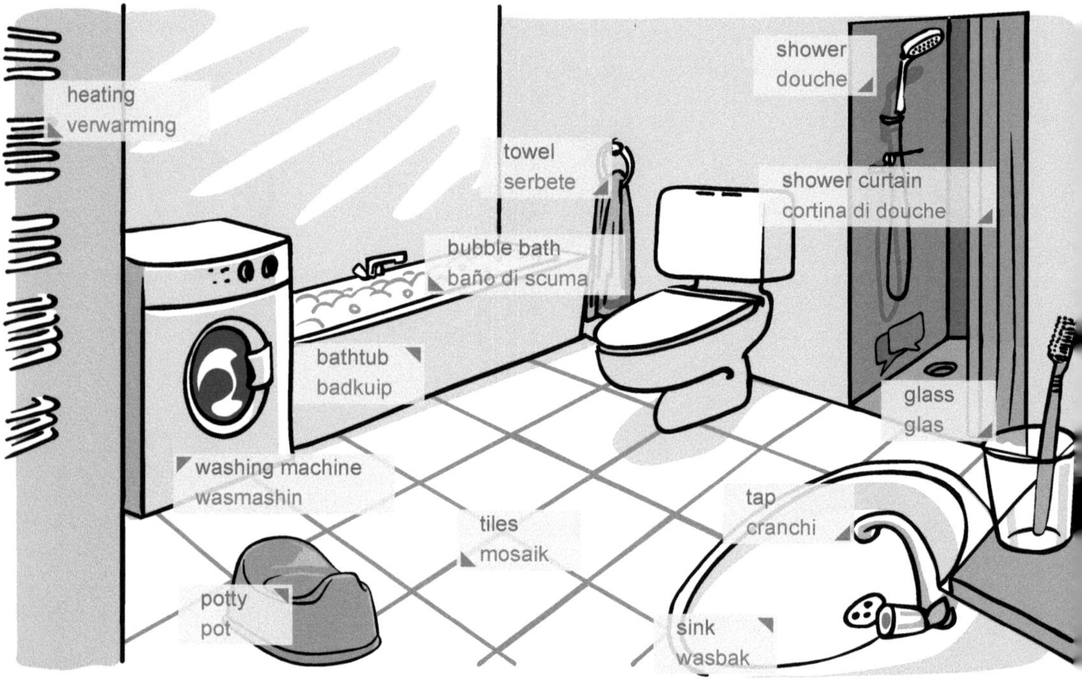

heating
verwarming
towel
serbete
shower
douche
shower curtain
cortina di douche
bubble bath
baño di scuma
bathtub
badkuip
glass
glas
washing machine
wasmashin
tap
cranchi
tiles
mosaik
potty
pot
sink
wasbak

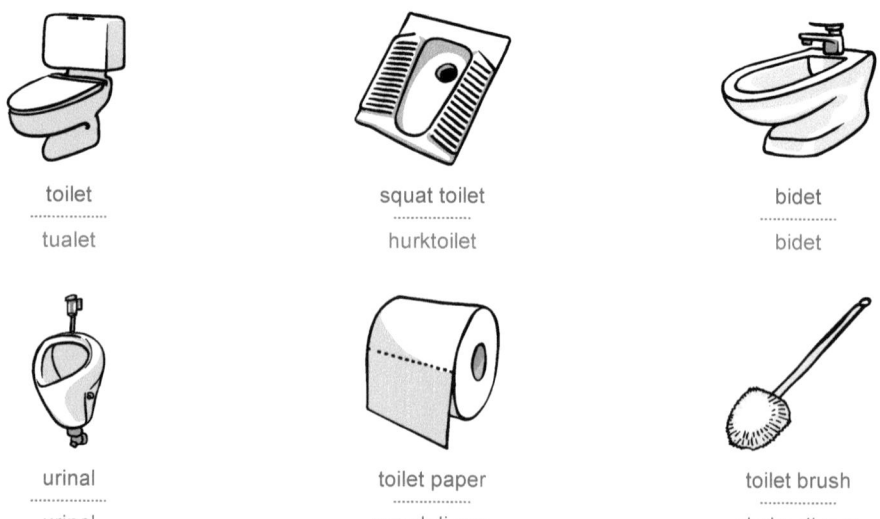

toilet

tualet

squat toilet

hurktoilet

bidet

bidet

urinal

urinal

toilet paper

papel di w.c.

toilet brush

skeiro di w.c.

toothbrush

skeiro di djente

toothpaste

pasta di djente

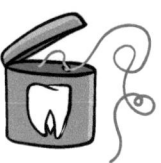

dental floss

dental floss

wash

laba

hand shower

douche di man

douche

bidet

basin

tobo

back brush

skeiro

soap

habon

shower gel

shower gel

shampoo

shampoo

flannel

washandje

drain

drain

creme

crema

deodorant

desodorante

mirror

spiel

hand mirror

spiel di man

razor

blet

shaving foam

shaving foam

aftershave

aftershave

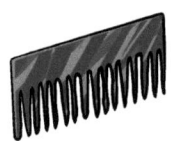

comb

peña

brush

skeiro

hair-dryer

blower

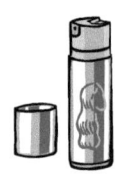

hairspray

spray pa cabey

makeup

makeup

lipstick

lipstick

nail varnish

cos di pinta huña

cotton wool

catuna

nail scissors

sker pa corta huña

perfume

perfume

bathroom - baño

washbag

tas

stool

kruk

weighing scales

balansa

bathrobe

bata

rubber gloves

handschoen

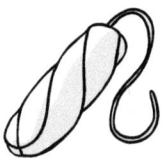

tampon

tampon

sanitary towel

kotex

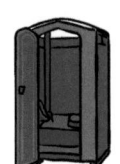

chemical toilet

wc kimico

kids room
camber di mucha

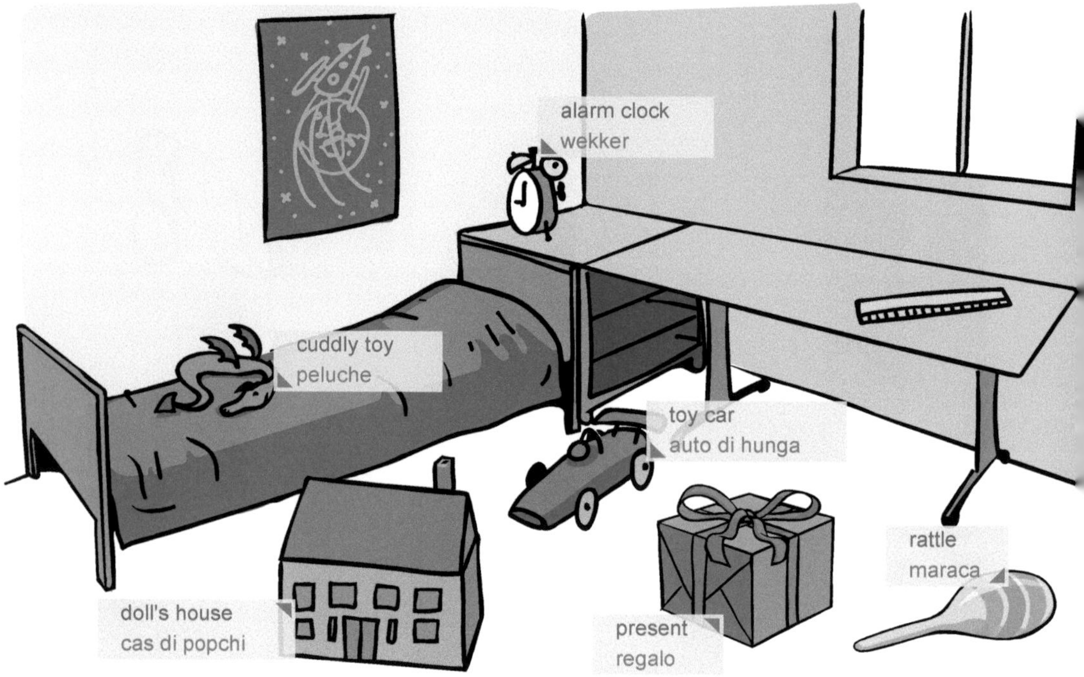

alarm clock
wekker
cuddly toy
peluche
toy car
auto di hunga
rattle
maraca
doll's house
cas di popchi
present
regalo

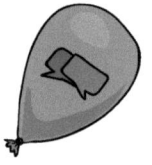

balloon
blaas

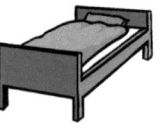

bed
cama

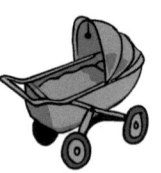

stroller
stroller

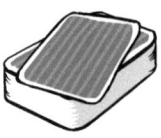

deck of cards
baraha di carta

jigsaw
puzzel

SUPER
MEGA

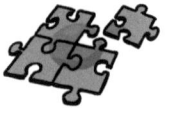

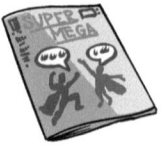

comic
comic

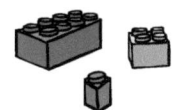

lego bricks

lego

toy blocks

bloki di hunga

action figure

figura di accion

romper suit

romper

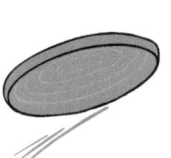

frisbee

frisbee

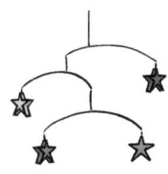

mobile

mobil

board game

wega di mesa

dice

dou

model train set

set di trein

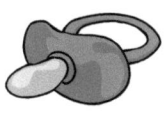

pacifier

chupon

party

fiesta

picture book

buki di prenchi

ball

bala

doll

popchi

play

hunga

sandpit

zandbak

swing

zoya

toys

cos di hunga

video game console

videogame

tricycle

tricycle

teddy bear

beer

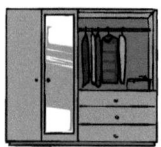

wardrobe

cashi di paña

clothing

paña

socks

mea

stockings

mea

tights

pantyhose

scarf
sjaal

belt
faha

umbrella
paraplu

t-shirt
T-shirt

boots
boots

slippers
slof

sneakers
keds

sandals	shoes	rubber boots
sandalia	sapato	laars di rubber

underwear	bra	undershirt
carsonsio	bh	flanel

body

body

pants

carson

jeans

jeans

skirt

saya

blouse

blusa

shirt

camisa

pullover

sweater

sweater

sweater

blazer

blazer

jacket

jacket

coat

jas

raincoat

regenjas

costume

flus

dress

shimis

wedding dress

shimis di bruid

suit

flus

nightgown

yapon

pajamas

pidjama

sari

sari

headscarf

lenso di cabes

turban

turban

burka

burqa

kaftan

kaftan

abaya

abaya

swimsuit

zwempak

trunks

zwembroek

shorts

carson cortico

tracksuit

trainingspak

apron

lantera

gloves

handschoen

button
boton

glasses
bril

bracelet
armband

necklace
cadena

ring
renchi

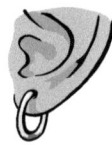

earring
renchi di horea

cap
pechi

coat hanger
kapstok

hat
sombre

tie
dashi

zip
ziper

helmet
helm

braces
guiel

school uniform
uniform di scol

uniform
uniform

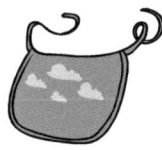

bib

babado

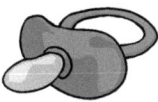

pacifier

chupon

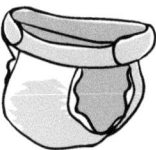

diaper

bruki

office
oficina

server
server
filing cabinet
filekast
printer
printer
paper
papel
monitor
pantaya
desk
lessenaar
mouse
mouse
folder
map
keyboard
keyboard
waste-paper basket
bari di sushi
chair
stoel
computer
computer

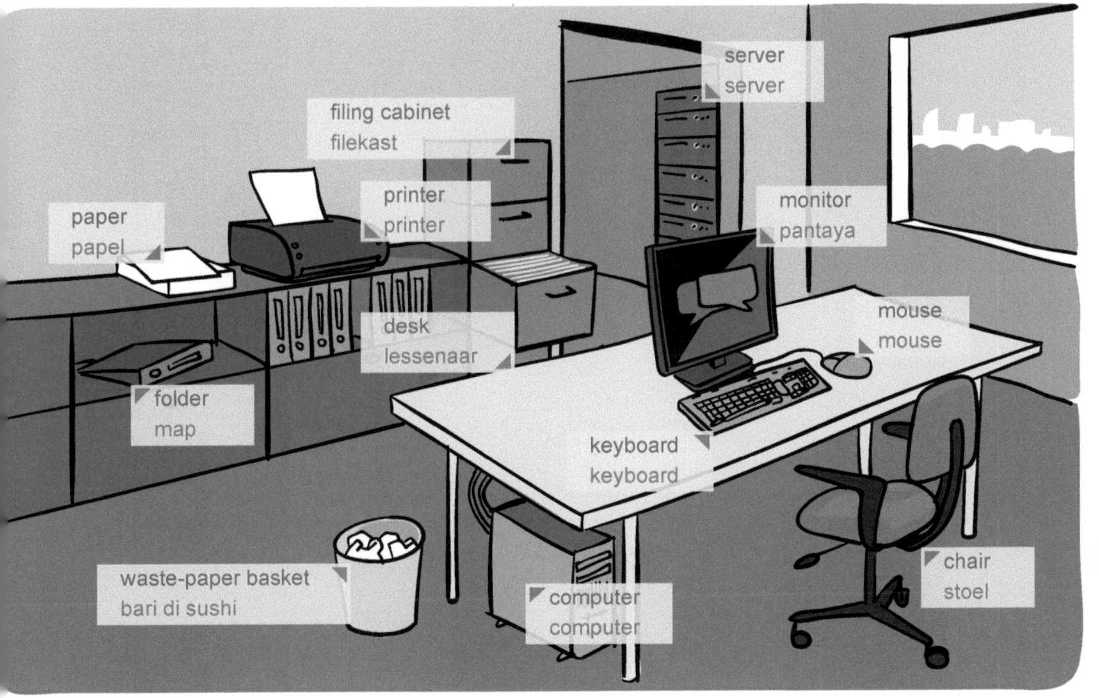

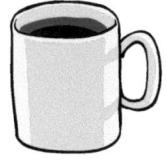

coffee mug

copi pa bebe koffie

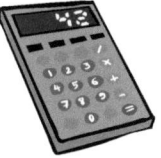

calculator

calculator

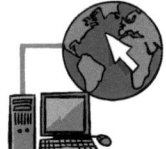

internet

internet

laptop

laptop

letter

carta

message

mensahe

cell phone

celular

network

red

photocopier

mashin di copia

software

software

telephone

telefon

plug socket

stopcontact

fax machine

fax mashin

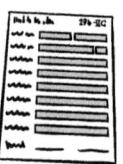

form

formulario

document

documento

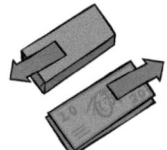

buy

cumpra

pay

paga

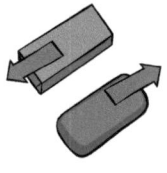

trade

negosha

money

placa

dollar

dollar

euro

euro

yen

yen

rouble

roebel

Swiss franc

frank suiso

renminbi yuan

yuan renminbi

rupee

roepi

cash point

bancomatico

currency exchange office

oficina di cambio

gold

oro

silver

plata

oil

azeta

energy

energia

price

prijs

contract

contract

tax

impuesto

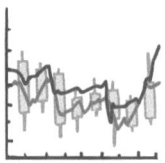

stock

share

work

traha

employee

empleado

employer

dunado di trabou

factory

fabrica

shop

tienda

police officer
agente policial

fireman
bombero

pilot
piloto

cook
coki

doctor
dokter

gardener

hardinero

carpenter

carpinte

seamstress

cosedo

judge

hues

chemist

kimico

actor

actor

bus driver

chauffeur di bus

taxi driver

chauffeur di taxi

fisherman

piscado

cleaning lady

hende cu ta haci cas limpi

roofer

drechado di dak

waiter

waiter

hunter

jaagdo

painter

verfdo

baker

panadero

electrician

electricista

builder

trahado den construccion

engineer

ingeniero

butcher

carnicero

plumber

loodgieter

postman

partido di carta

soldier

solda

architect

arkitecto

cashier

cahero

florist

florista

hairdresser

pelukero / pelukera

conductor

controlado di ticket

mechanic

mecanico

captain

capitan

dentist

dentista

scientist

cientifico

rabbi

rabbi

imam

imam

monk

monk

pastor

pastor

tools
herment

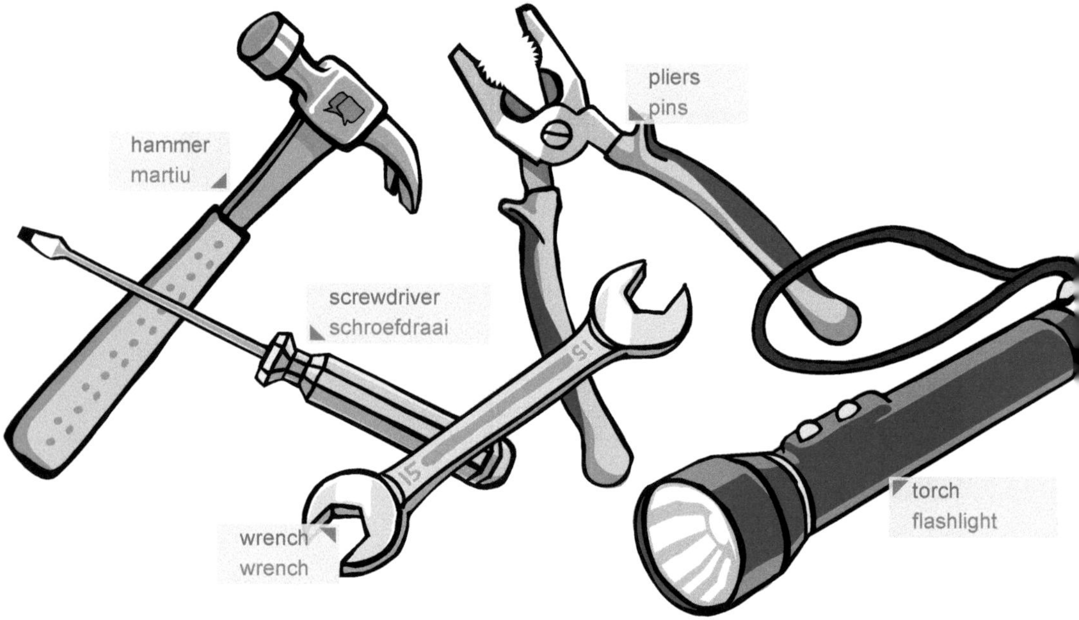
hammer
martiu
pliers
pins
screwdriver
schroefdraai
wrench
wrench
torch
flashlight

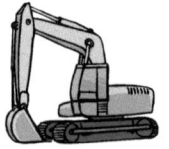

excavator

bulldozer

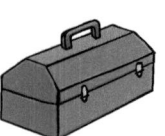

toolbox

caha di herment

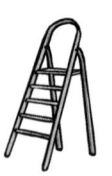

ladder

trapi

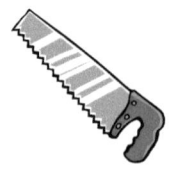

saw

zaag

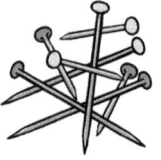

nails

clabo

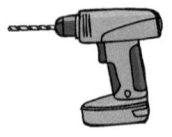

drill

boormashin

repair
drecha

shovel
shobel

Damn!
caraho!

dustpan
scop

paint can
bleki di verf

screws
schroef

musical instruments
instrumento musical

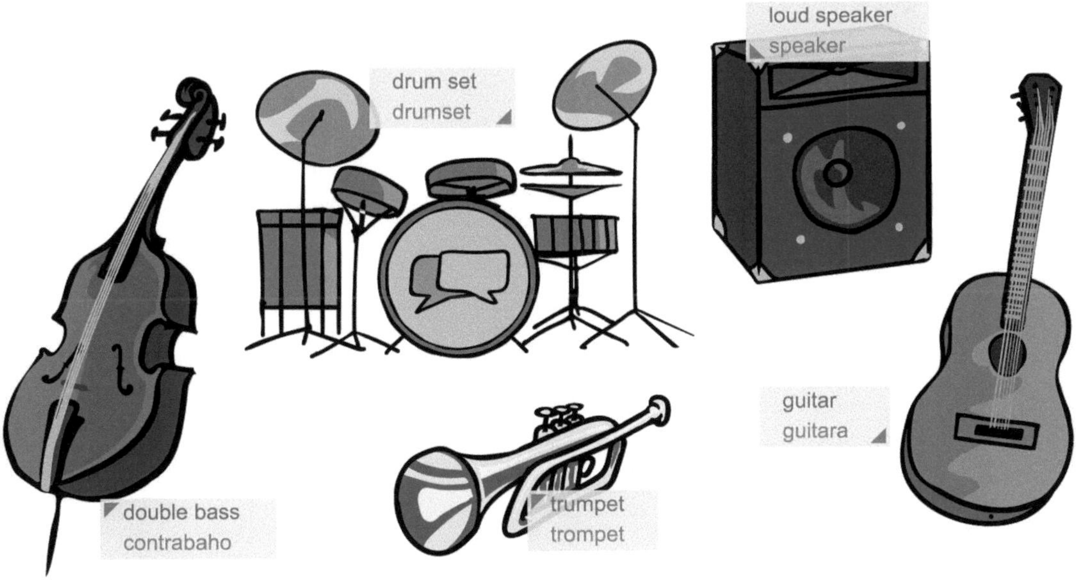

double bass
contrabaho

drum set
drumset

loud speaker
speaker

guitar
guitara

trumpet
trompet

piano

piano

violin

fio

bass

baho

timpani

timbal

drums

tambu

keyboard

keyboard

saxophone

saxofon

flute

fluit

microphone

microfon

musical instruments - instrumento musical

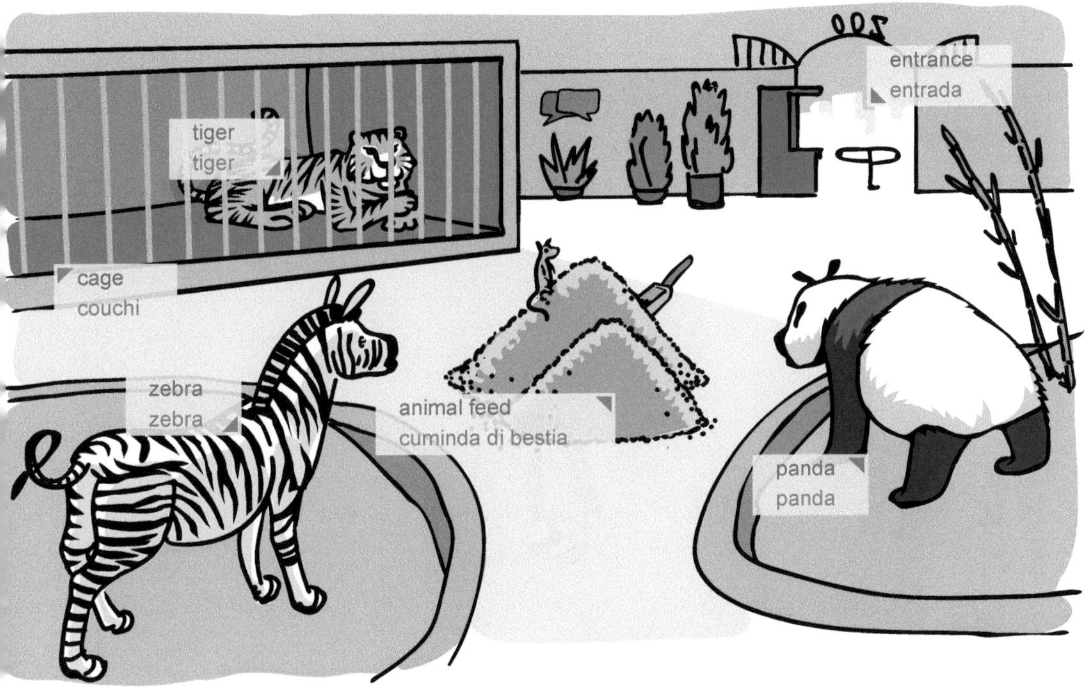

entrance
entrada

tiger
tiger

cage
couchi

zebra
zebra

animal feed
cuminda di bestia

panda
panda

animals
animal

elephant
olifante

kangaroo
cangaru

rhino
neushoorn

gorilla
gorila

bear
beer

camel

camel

ostrich

avestruz

lion

leon

monkey

macaco

flamingo

flamingo

parrot

lora

polar bear

beer polar

penguin

pinguin

shark

tribon

peacock

pauwies

snake

colebra

crocodile

caiman

zookeeper

cuidado di bestia

seal

cacho di awa

jaguar

jaguar

pony
pony

leopard
leopardo

hippo
hipopotamo

giraffe
giraf

eagle
aguila

boar
porco di mondi

fish
pisca

turtle
turtuga

walrus
walrus

fox
vos

gazelle
gazelle

American football
futbol Americano

cycling
ciclismo

tennis
tennis

basketball
basketball

swimming
landamento

boxing
boxeo

ice hockey
ice hockey

soccer
futbol

badminton
badminton

athletics
atletismo

handball
handbal

skiing
ski

polo
polo

laugh
hari

jump
bula

hug
brasa

walk
cana

sing
canta

dream
soña

pray
resa

kiss
sunchi

write
skirbi

draw
pinta

show
mustra

push
primi

give
duna

take
coy

have
tin

do
haci

be
ta

stand
para

run
core

pull
ranca

throw
tira

fall
cay

lie
drumi

wait
warda

carry
carga

sit
sinta

get dressed
bisti

sleep
drumi

wake up
lanta fo'i soño

look at

mira

cry

yora

stroke

caricia

comb

peña

talk

papia

understand

compronde

ask

puntra

listen

scucha

drink

bebe

eat

come

tidy up

ruim op

love

stima

cook

cushna

drive

bai

fly

bula

sail

zeilo

calculate

conta

read

lesa

learn

siña

work

traha

marry

casa

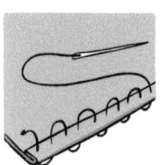

sew

cose

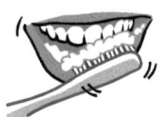

brush teeth

skeiro djente

kill

mata

smoke

huma

send

manda

family
famia

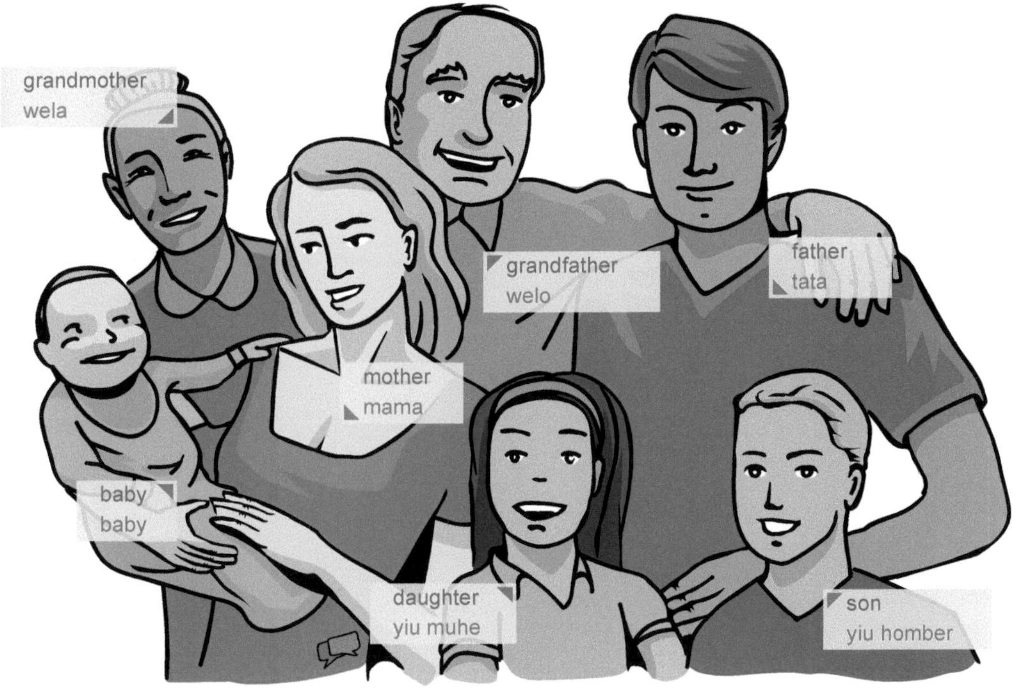
grandmother
wela
grandfather
welo
father
tata
mother
mama
baby
baby
daughter
yiu muhe
son
yiu homber

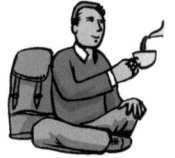

guest
huesped

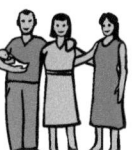

aunt
tanta

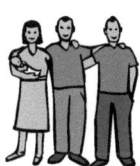

uncle
omo

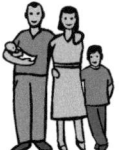

brother
ruman homber

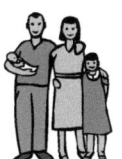

sister
ruman muhe

body

curpa

forehead
frenta
eye
wowo
shoulder
schouder
finger
dede
face
cara
chin
cachete
hand
man
leg
pia
breast
pecho
arm
brasa

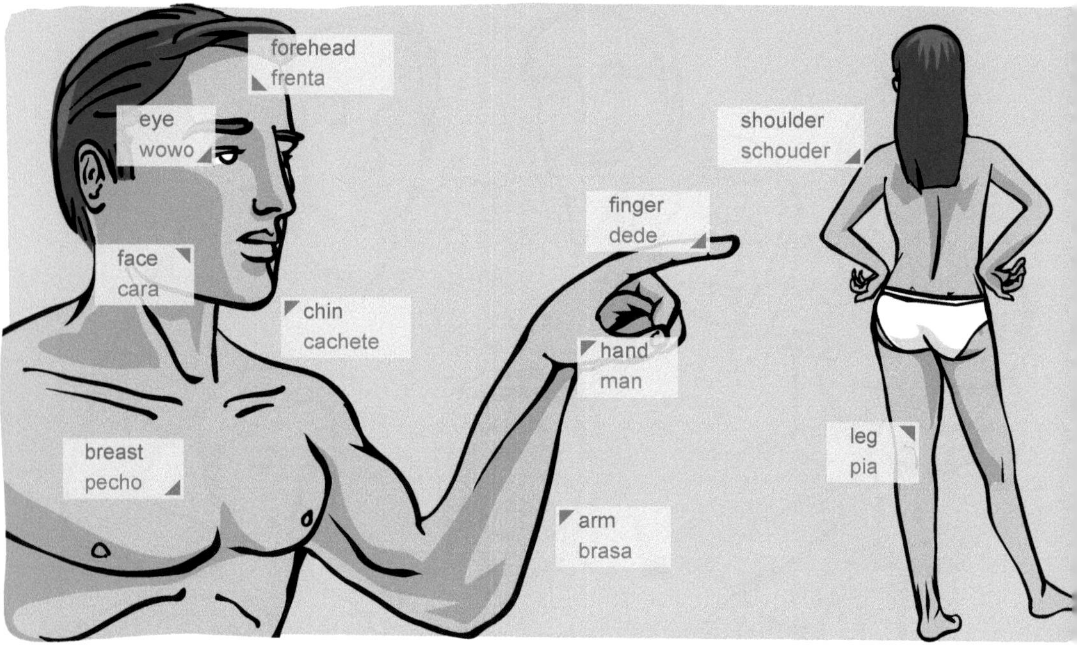

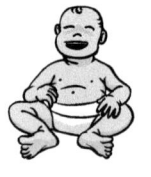

baby
baby

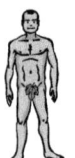

man
homber

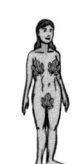

woman
muhe

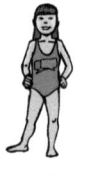

girl
mucha muhe

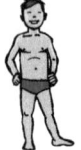

boy
mucha homber

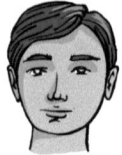

head
cabes

back

lomba

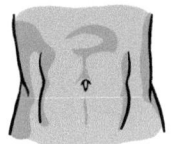

belly

bariga

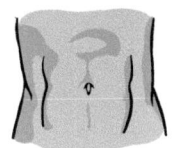

navel

lombrishi

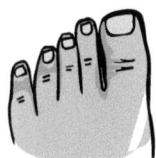

toe

dede di pia

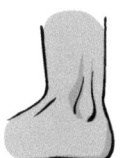

heel

hilchi

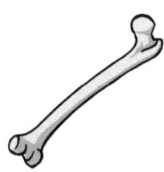

bone

weso

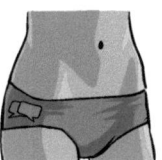

hip

heup

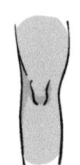

knee

rudia

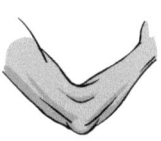

elbow

elleboog

nose

nanishi

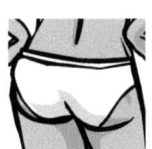

buttocks

chanchan

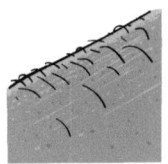

skin

cuero

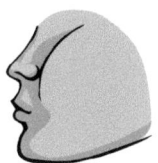

cheek

wang

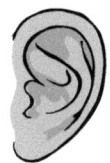

ear

horea

lip

lip

mouth

boca

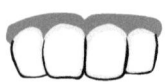

tooth

djente

tongue

lenga

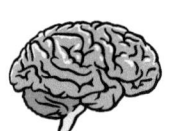

brain

celebro

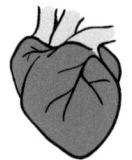

heart

curason

muscle

musculo

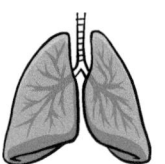

lung

pulmon

liver

higra

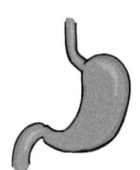

stomach

stoma

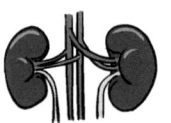

kidneys

nier

sex

sex

condom

condon

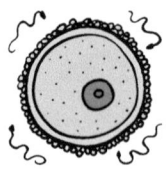

ovum

ovulo

semen

sperma

pregnancy

embaraso

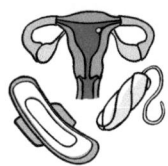

menstruation

menstruacion

vagina

vagina

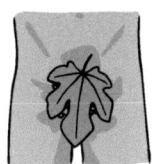

penis

penis

eyebrow

wenkbrauw

hair

cabey

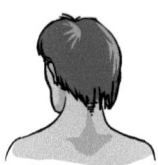

neck

nek

hospital
hospital

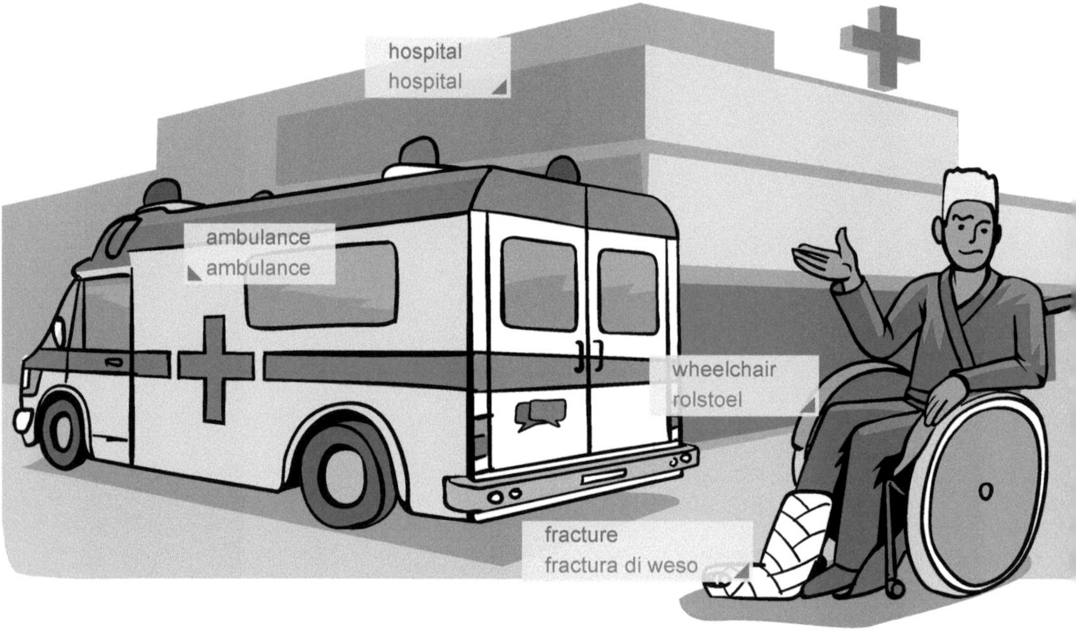

hospital
hospital
ambulance
ambulance
wheelchair
rolstoel
fracture
fractura di weso

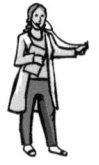

doctor

dokter

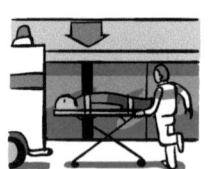

emergency room

EHBO (prome asistencia/eerste hulp)

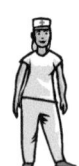

nurse

nurse

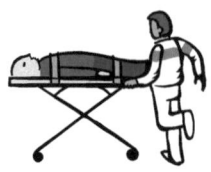

emergency

caso di emergencia

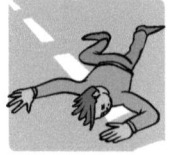

unconscious

fo'i tino

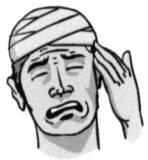

pain

dolor

injury

lesion

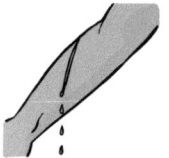

bleeding

sangramento

heart attack

ataca di curason

stroke

ataca celebral

allergy

alergia

cough

tosa

fever

keintura

flu

griep

diarrhea

diarea

headache

dolor di cabes

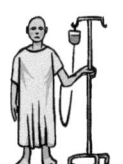

cancer

cancer

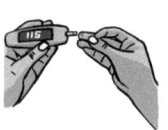

diabetes

diabetes

surgeon

ciruhano

scalpel

scalpel

operation

operacion

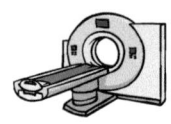

CT
CT

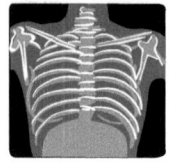

x-ray
x-ray

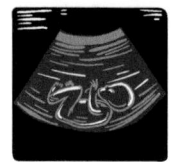

ultrasound
echo

face mask
masker contra stof

disease
malesa

waiting room
sala di espera

crutch
kruk

plaster
pleister

bandage
verband

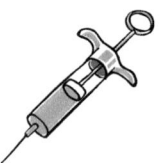

injection
inyeccion

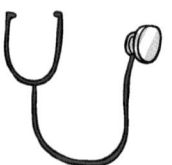

stethoscope
stetoscop

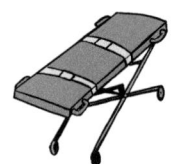

stretcher
brancard

clinical thermometer
thermometer

birth
nacemento

overweight
sobrepeso

hearing aid

aparato pa oido

disinfectant

desinfectante

infection

infeccion

virus

virus

HIV / AIDS

HIV / AIDS

medicine

remedi

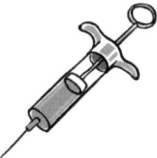

vaccination

vacuna

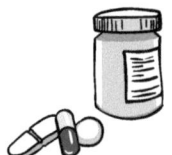

tablets

pilder

pill

pilder

emergency call

yamada di emergencia

blood pressure monitor

aparato pa midi presion

ill / healthy

malo / saludabel

Help!

auxilio!

alarm

alarma

assault

atraco

attack

atake

danger

peliger

emergency exit

salida di emergencia

Fire!

candela

fire extinguisher

brandspuit

accident

desgracia

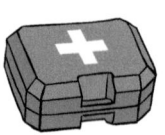

first-aid kit

caha di prome asistencia

SOS

SOS

police

polis

Europe

Europa

North America

Noord America

South America

Sur America

Africa

Africa

Asia

Asia

Australia

Australia

Atlantic

Oceano Atlantico

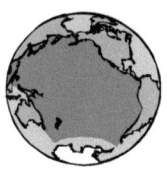

Pacific

Oceano Pacifico

Indian Ocean

Oceano Indio

Antarctic Ocean

Oceano Antartico

Arctic Ocean

Oceano Artico

North pole

Noordpool

South pole

Zuidpool

Antarctica

Antartica

earth

mundo

land

tera

sea

lama

island

isla

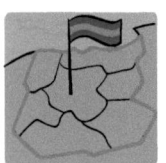

nation

nacion

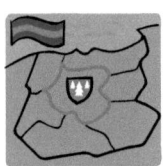

state

estado

clock face

holoshi analog

hour hand

wijzer chikito

minute hand

wijzer grandi

second hand

wijzer di seconde

What time is it?

Cuant'or tin?

day

dia

time

tempo

now

awor

digital watch

holoshi digital

minute

minuut

hour

ora

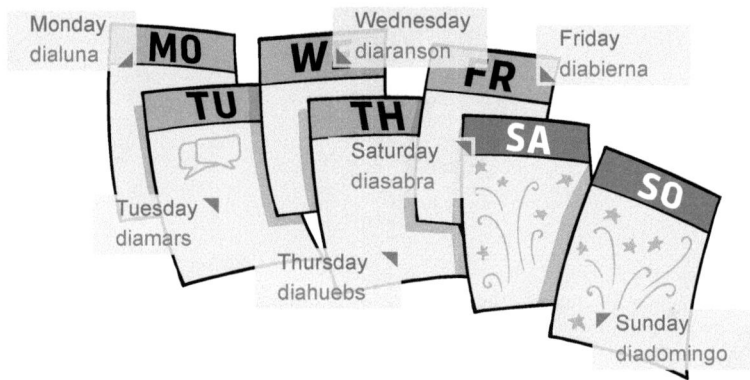

Monday
dialuna

Wednesday
diaranson

Friday
diabierna

Tuesday
diamars

Saturday
diasabra

Thursday
diahuebs

Sunday
diadomingo

yesterday

ayera

today

awe

tomorrow

mañan

morning

mainta

noon

merdia

evening

anochi

workdays

dia di trabou

weekend

weekend

year
aña

rain
awacero
rainbow
arco iris
wind
biento
snow
sneeuw
spring
lente
fall
herfst
summer
zomer
winter
winter

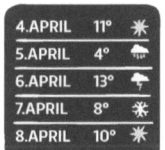

4.APRIL 11°
5.APRIL 4°
6.APRIL 13°
7.APRIL 8°
8.APRIL 10°

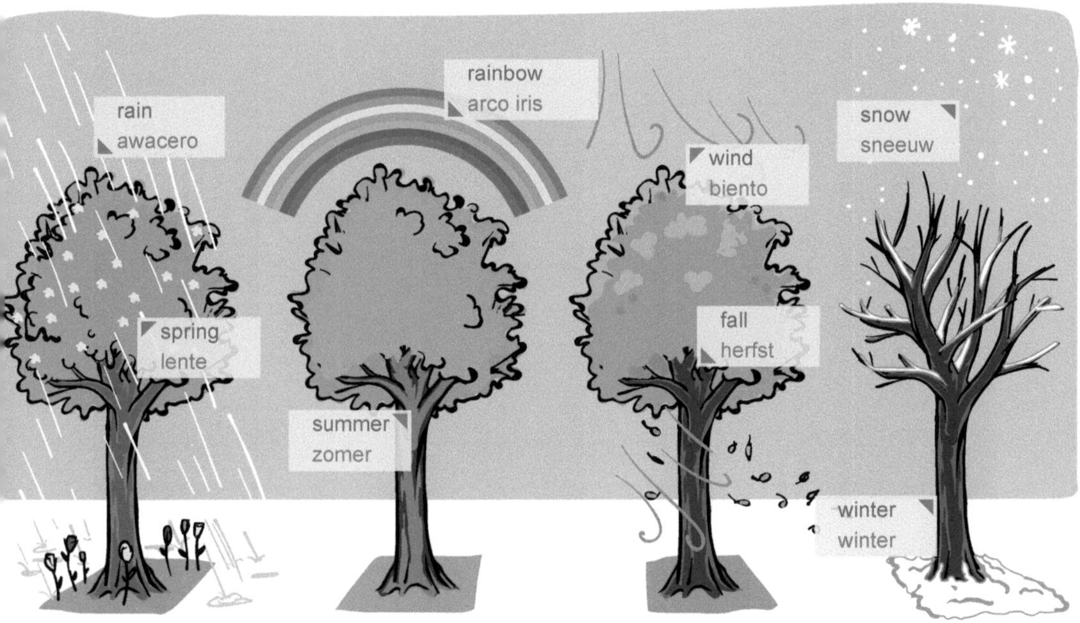

weather forecast

pronostico di tempo

F C
120 90 60 30 0 -30
40 30 20 10 0 -10 -20

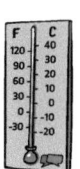

thermometer

thermometer

sunshine

solo ta briya

cloud

nubia

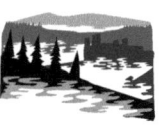

fog

neblina

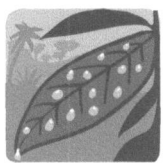

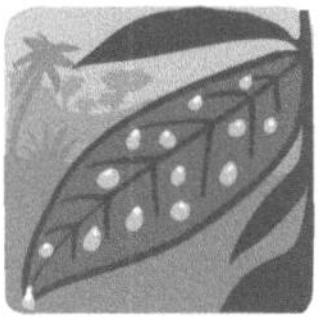

humidity

humedad

lightning

lamper

thunder

strena

storm

mal tempo

hail

hagel

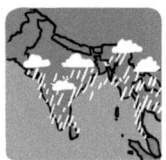

monsoon

mal tempo

flood

inundacion

ice

ijs

January

januari

February

februari

March

maart

April

april

May

mei

June

juni

July

juli

August

augustus

year - aña

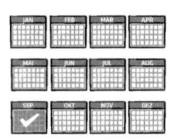

September
....
september

October
....
october

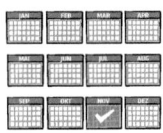

November
....
november

December
....
december

circle
....
circulo

square
....
cuadra

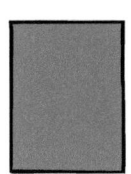

rectangle
....
rectangulo

triangle
....
triangulo

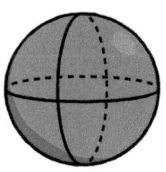

sphere
....
bol

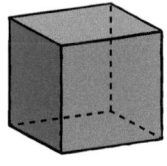

cube
....
kubus

white

blanco

yellow

geel

orange

oraño

pink

ros

red

cora

purple

biña

blue

blauw

green

berde

brown

bruin

gray

shinishi

black

preto

a lot / a little
....
hopi / tiki

angry / calm
....
rabia / trankil

beautiful / ugly
....
bunita / mahos

beginning / end
....
comienso / final

big / small
....
grandi / chikito

bright / dark
....
cla / scur

brother / sister
....
ruman homber / ruman
muhe

clean / dirty
....
limpi / sushi

complete / incomplete
....
completo / incompleto

day / night
....
dia / anochi

dead / alive
....
morto / bibo

wide / narrow
....
hancho / smal

edible / inedible

comibel / incomibel

evil / kind

mal hende / bon hende

excited / bored

ansioso / ferfela bo mes

fat / thin

gordo / flaco

first / last

prome / ultimo

friend / enemy

amigo / enemigo

full / empty

yen / bashi

hard / soft

duro / moli

heavy / light

pisa / lihe

hunger / thirst

hamber / sed

ill / healthy

malo / saludabel

illegal / legal

ilegal / legal

intelligent / stupid

inteligente / sabi

left / right

robes / drechi

near / far

cerca / leu

new / used
nobo / uza

nothing / something
nada / algo

old / young
bieu / jong

on / off
cendi / paga

open / closed
habri / cera

quiet / loud
keto / duro

rich / poor
rico / pober

right / wrong
bon / fout

rough / smooth
grof / liso

sad / happy
tristo / contento

short / long
cortico / largo

slow / fast
pocopoco / lihe

wet / dry
muha / seco

warm / cool
cayente / friu

war / peace
guera / paz

0

zero

cero

1

one

un

2

two

dos

3

three

tres

4

four

cuater

5

five

cinco

6

six

seis

7

seven

shete

8

eight

ocho

9

nine

nuebe

10

ten

dies

11

eleven

diesun

12

twelve

diesdos

13

thirteen

diestres

14

fourteen

diescuatro

15

fifteen

diescinco

16

sixteen

diesseis

17

seventeen

diesshete

18

eighteen

diesocho

19

nineteen

diesnuebe

20

twenty

binti

100

hundred

shen

1.000

thousand

mil

1.000.000

million

miyon

English
Ingles

American English
Ingles Mericano

Chinese Mandarin
Chines Mandarin

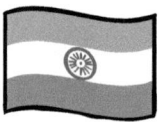

Hindi
Hindi

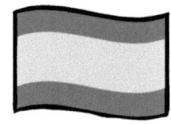

Spanish
Spaño

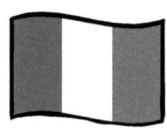

French
Frances

Arabic
Arabe

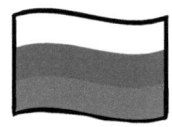

Russian
Ruso

Portuguese
Portugues

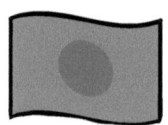

Bengali
Bengal

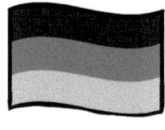

German
Aleman

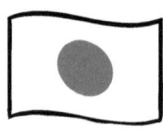

Japanese
Hapones

I
ami

you
abo

he / she / it
e

we
nos

you
boso

they
nan

who?
ken?

what?
kico?

how?
con?

where?
unda?

when?
ki ora?

name
nomber

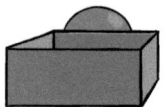

behind

patras

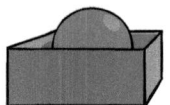

in

den

in front of

dilanti di

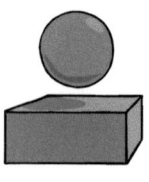

over

ariba

on

riba

under

bou di

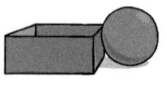

beside

banda di

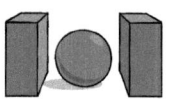

between

entre

place

luga